D0516037

CALGARY PUBLIC LIBRARY

JUL - 2012

# OPEN WIDE!

Cataloging Information

Ham, Catherine.
    Open wide! : a look inside animal mouths /Catherine Ham
        32 p. : col. ill. ; 20 cm.
    Includes index (p.).
    Summary: Uses verse and photographs to explore the
mouths of animals. Includes a range of taxa, including mammals,
amphibians, birds, reptiles, molluscs, and fish.

    LC: QL 857 .H35 2012
    Dewey: 573.3
    ISBN-13: 978-0-9832014-3-4   (alk. paper)
        Mouth—Juvenile literature
        Animals—habits and behavior

Cover Design: Stewart Pack
Art Director: Celia Naranjo
Copy Editor: Tina Miller
Photo Research: Dawn Cusick
Production Assistance: Jackie Kerr


10 9 8 7 6 5 4 3 2 1

First edition

Published by EarlyLight Books, Inc.
1436 Dellwood Road
Waynesville, NC  28786

Text Copyright © 2012 Catherine Ham

Manufactured in China in September, 2011.
All rights reserved.

ISBN-13: 978-0-9832014-3-4

To Lucia . . .

# OPEN WIDE!

## A Look Inside Animal Mouths

## Catherine Ham

 EarlyLight Books

WAYNESVILLE, NORTH CAROLINA, USA

# OPEN WIDE!

Some yawning, some yowling
Mouths of all sizes
Some so ginormous
They'll surely win prizes!

Huge teeth, tiny teeth
Teeth to crush and grind
Big mouths, mini mouths
Trying food to find

# NAP TIME!

Oh dear! What's going on here?
Is he tired? Unhappy?
Something to fear?

What's he saying?
He's been playing?
Maybe you can hear

Play is a serious business
It's how lion cubs learn
How to fight and how to hunt
And how to wait their turn

How did the prairie dog get its name?
It's a burrowing type of squirrel
And a dog is not the same

They live in family groups
And each group has a guard
It's his job to warn of danger
Which he does by barking hard

The guard checks out a predator
From his look-out on a mound
The others dive down their burrows
Till he gives the "All clear!" sound

# ALARM CALL!

There are many types of otters
Mostly they eat fish
They'll steal an eel
Or grab a crab
Frogs are a tasty dish

Otters bite and crush their food
They are not fools
Use rocks as tools
To peel a meal
From clams tight glued

Acrobatic in the water
Energetic as you please
The sleekly streamlined otter
Hide-and-seeking otter
Dives and swims with ease

# SWEET TOOTH

# GO AWAY!

**LEAVE!**

A face that's masked
A tail with rings
They feed at night
And eat most things

This one here's
Not happy though
Why's he upset?
Do you know?

# RIBBIT!

Open wide!
Can you see my teeth inside?
That's because they're not like yours
I don't have two rows in my jaws
It's not my teeth that grab my meal
I use my sticky tongue to reel
Into my mouth what I can catch
Some fly I nab, or moth I snatch
Instead I have weak upper teeth
To grind my food up as I eat

## RAZOR
## TEETH!

Bats are the only mammals that can fly
They whizz around, zapping bugs
In the night-dark sky
They have lots of tiny teeth
Sleep hanging by their feet
Not something we can do, you and I

# YABBER! JABBER!

Monkeys live in groups
So they need to get along
Howling and nattering
Yowling and chattering
They are noisy all day long

There are many types of monkeys
All of them are primates
Some are humongous
And some are flyweights
But whether big or small
Monkeys love to screech and call

SURPRISE!

This red-ruffed lemur's
Great big eyes
Make him look
So surprised

His huge great eyes
Collect the light
With special cells
To see at night
His huge great eyes
Reflect the light
Which means
He can be seen
At night

If he's been seen
Could that be why
This guy's mouth
Is open wide......?
YOU DECIDE
But let's respect
His need to hide

# STAND BACK!

Zebras are herbivores
It's mainly grass they eat
Their front teeth cut
The back teeth grind

In drought, when grass
Is hard to find
Then shrubs and twigs
And bark and leaves
Are a hunger-busting treat

With their eyes on the side
Zebras see far and wide
Their beautiful stripes
Help them safely to hide

Would you believe
That a creature
So huge and so tall
Would have a mouth
Which in fact is quite small?

What is he doing here?
Yawning?
Or making some sound?
If he's taking a sleep
Won't he lie on the ground?

Can he keep standing
Be asleep on his feet?
Did you know that he can?
Isn't that neat!

## LOUD MOUTH!

# CAN YOU SPOT ME?

A mouth that is big
A jaw that is strong
Front teeth that can pierce
Sharp-pointed and long

They hunt mainly at night
Stalking close to their prey
Which they haul up a tree
To keep meat thieves away

# BIG NOISE!

This hippo's one furious fellow
What a ferocious great bellow
A mouth so titanic
With teeth so gigantic
You know that he doesn't eat Jell-o!

If you happen to meet
This chap on the street
There's no need to panic
No need to get frantic...
You won't be his treat
Plants are all that he'll eat

What a mouth, goodness me!
Opened wide, you can see
All the way inside

Is he growling, yowling, howling?
Don't think so... no....
He's sure not scowling

If that's a yawn with all his might
Would his eyes be scrunched up tight?
You decide

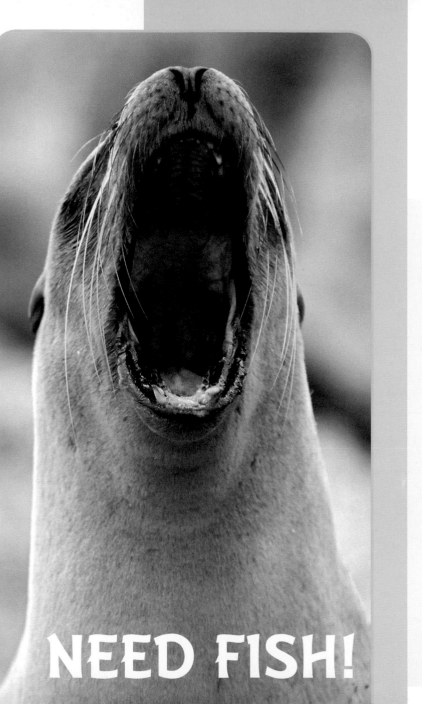

**NEED FISH!**

SNAP!
GOTCHA!

The turtle is a reptile
Some live in water
Some on land
And with his house
Upon his back
His life is pretty grand

A turtle's mouth
Is different
It's not like mine or yours
First off, it has no teeth
But extremely hard, strong jaws

And once these jaws
Have snapped shut
Tightly on some prey
There's no way
For that turtle's meal
To ever get away

19

# CAN'T FLY? DON'T CRY!

The penguin is a bird
Which cannot fly
And a bird has no teeth
Which is why
What you see in this mouth
Are toothlike barbs
A kind of backward-pointing hook
Just as jagged as they look
Which grip the slippery prey
And help it on its way
Down the gullet
To the stomach
Further south!

# SCREECH!

Can you tell if this seagull is furious?
Could it be that she simply is curious?
Is her mouth shouting: "NO!"
Is she just saying: "Oh?"
We don't know....
It's all very mysterious

# FEED ME!

Baby birds have special mouths
Which open very wide
So when the parents bring food
They can drop a lot inside

The mouth is brightly colored
So the parents cannot miss
When you sit down for dinner
Please don't cheep like this!

Can the ostrich see you?
His eyesight's very good
Did you, like I
Know he can't fly?
With those wings
You'd think he could

And why's his mouth wide open?
Is it because he's hot?
He pants to cool himself down
One of the ways he's got

**HEY THERE!**

SLOBBERER!

These are the world's largest lizards
You can't say they're pretty at all
Their mouths are constantly drooling
A slimy slobber waterfall

Their mouths are so awfully filthy
A dentist would freak if he saw
The millions and trillions of germs
All over their teeth and their jaw

For the longest time scientists thought
Germs sickened their prey so it died
But now their studies have shown them
Komodo teeth have poison inside

Doesn't this look like a huge happy smile
Filling the face of a toothy crocodile?
Actually, it's not
It's the only way he's got
Of cooling down

Scaly crocodiles can't sweat
And let us not forget
They live in a spot
Where it's always very hot
With water pooling all around

**CRUNCH & MUNCH**

The wide open mouth's his style
Of throwing off the heat a while

25

**EEL MEAL!**

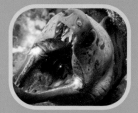

An eel is a very long
And slender fish
But I wish
People wouldn't make
The mistake
Of thinking it's a snake

Eels hide in rocks and reefs
And have a most unusual way
Of grabbing prey

An eel has no paws
So he can't use any claws
But the mouth of an eel
Has two sets of jaws
Both with teeth...
Good grief!

This file clam is a mollusc
And has a two-part shell
Which often stays wide open
It can't close tight very well

The brightly colored tentacles
Have a wriggly, wiggly knack
To scare a passing predator
Who may be thinking of a snack

File clams suck in water
To filter food to eat
It also brings in oxygen
To make their lives complete

PLENTIFUL
TENTACLES

POP IN!

This predator fish
Picks no special dish
Though he thinks
Crab and lobster
Are really quite delish

With one swish of water
Through his great gills
Whole into his mouth
Each tasty snack he swills

Mister Grouper is no wimp
But he loves his cleaner shrimp
For these dentists of the Seas
Clean his nasty teeth with ease

# OPEN WIDER!

SNAP!

TRAPPED!

The crocodile fish has a very flat head
He likes to lie in waiting, playing dead
Among the sand and the rocks
Of a shallow seabed

He's a master of disguise
Even camo's up his eyes
And when he spies
Some tasty fishy prize . . .
Then his huge mouth opens wide
To trap the ambushed prey inside

29

PELICANS

FRINGEHEAD FISH

TEGU LIZARD

CAMEL

DOLPHIN

BEAR

PEACOCK

ORANGUTAN

LEOPARD GECKOS

TIGER

# INDEX

## Acknowledgments

**Photography by:** John A. Anderson, Geanina Bechea, P. Borowka, Clickit, Vladyslav Danilin, David Evison, Four Oaks, Chris Fourie, Vlad Gavriloff, Vasyl Helevachuk, Song Heming, Eric Isselée, Marcel Jancovic, Natalie Jean, Cathy Keifer, Olga Khoroshunova, Yuriy Korchagin, Ivan Kuzmin, Eduard Kyslynskyy, George Lamson, Brian Lasenby, Peter Leahy, Kravchenko Marina, Nagel Photography, Photobar, Dr. Paul J. Polechla, Maxim S. Pometun, Uryadnikov Sergey, Becky Sheridan, Shutterstock Images, Audrey Snider-Bell, Jens Stolt, Stuart Taylor, Anne Tje, Gerrit de Vries, David Young, and Alex Zabusik.

**Gratitude** is also extended to the American Wildlife Foundation, Capital Regional District (Vancouver Island), Carole Dennis, Michael Dennis, National Geographic, Otternet, Jay Sharp, Dr. Michael Stuart, Dr. Stephen Wroe, www.australian-animals.net, and www.wildmadagascar.org /wildlife/lemurs.